Explore Ancient Egypt

Zelda Wagner

Lerner Publications ◆ Minneapolis

Lerner Publications Company
An imprint of Lerner Publishing Group, Inc.
241 First Avenue North
Minneapolis, MN 55401 USA

For reading levels and more information, look up this title at www.lernerbooks.com.

Main body text set in Billy Infant Regular. Typeface provided by SparkyType.

Editor: Evan Villas

Library of Congress Cataloging-in-Publication Data

Names: Wagner, Zelda, 2000- author
Title: Explore Ancient Egypt / Zelda Wagner.
Description: Minneapolis: Lerner Publications, [2026] | Series: Lightning Bolt Books. Early civilizations | Includes bibliographical references and index. | Audience: Ages 6-9 | Audience: Grades 2-3 | Summary: "Who built the pyramids? What did ancient Egyptians do for fun? Readers uncover these questions and more as they travel through time to explore the awesome world of ancient Egypt"— Provided by publisher.
Identifiers: LCCN 2025012269 (print) | LCCN 2025012270 (ebook) | ISBN 9798765689240 lib. bdg. | ISBN 9798348028930 pbk | ISBN 9798765696668 epub
Subjects: LCSH: Egypt—Civilization—332 B.C.-638 A.D. | Egypt—Antiquities—Juvenile literature
Classification: LCC DT60 .W323 2026 (print) | LCC DT60 (ebook) | DDC 932—dc23/eng/20250602

LC record available at https://lccn.loc.gov/2025012269
LC ebook record available at https://lccn.loc.gov/2025012270

Manufactured in the United States of America
1-1012501-54792-4/22/2025

Table of Contents

The Ancient Egyptians 4

Egyptian Life 10

The End of Egypt 18

A Look at the Great Pyramid of Giza 20

Ancient Egypt Facts 21

Glossary 22

Learn More 23

Index 24

The Ancient Egyptians

About five thousand years ago, ancient Egypt was growing. This society existed along the Nile River in northeast Africa for thousands of years.

Ancient Egyptians were skilled farmers and builders. They built pyramids and monuments.

Egypt has a harsh, hot desert climate. **Little rain falls there.**

The Pyramids at Giza have been standing for almost five thousand years.

The Nile River flows for more than 4,000 miles (6,400 km) through northeast Africa. The river provided Egyptians with almost everything they needed.

Strong animals such as oxen helped farmers plow the fields.

Egyptians grew crops such as wheat and barley near the river. They caught fish from its waters.

Ancient Egypt
MEDITERRANEAN SEA
Great Pyramid of Giza
Giza
AFRICA
Nile River
RED SEA
Ancient Egypt
City
River

Egyptian Life

Some Egyptians used a writing system called hieroglyphics. It included an alphabet of more than seven hundred different pictures. Scribes trained for years to read and write hieroglyphics.

Daily life in Egypt depended on one's class. Enslaved people lived the harshest lives. They did the hardest jobs.

Farmers and craftspeople worked hard too. Farmers planted crops. Craftspeople made pots, clothing, and other goods.

Pottery was decorated with hieroglyphics.

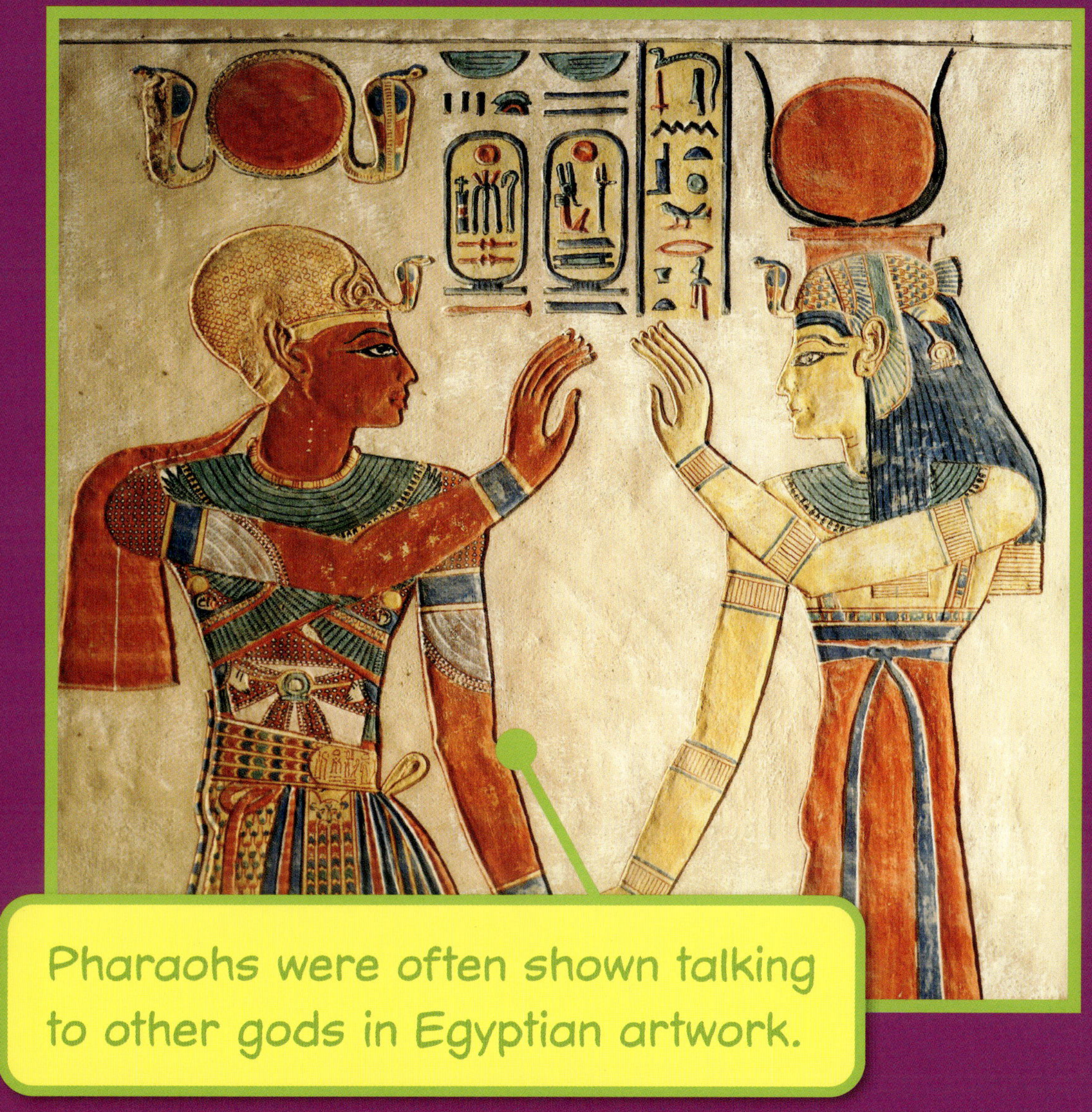

Pharaohs were often shown talking to other gods in Egyptian artwork.

Nobles were the highest class. Among them was Egypt's king, or pharaoh. **The pharaoh was considered a god.**

Ancient Egyptians believed gods controlled life in Egypt. Many gods were part human, part animal. The god Anubis had the body of a human and the head of a dog.

Anubis was the ancient Egyptian god of the dead.

The tombs of pharaohs were filled with treasures such as jewelry and weapons.

Ancient Egyptians also thought people needed their bodies after they died. So they preserved bodies with oils and beeswax and wrapped them with linen. The bodies were buried in tombs.

Egyptians enjoyed art and music in their spare time. They attended festivals. A board game called senet was popular.

This senet board was found in the tomb of the pharaoh Tutankhamen, or King Tut.

Some ancient Egyptians kept pets. **Egyptians thought cats were gods in disguise.** Some owners even preserved their cat's body after it died.

Craftspeople made sculptures of cats.

The End of Egypt

Egypt faced a series of attacks beginning in the 700s BCE. It faced famine and drought over the next centuries.

Alexander the Great built the city of Alexandria in northern Egypt.

Alexander the Great of Greece took over Egypt in 332 BCE. Three hundred years later, the Roman Empire took over Egypt again. This was the true end of ancient Egypt.

A Look at the Great Pyramid of Giza

The Great Pyramid of Giza was a huge tomb. It was the tallest structure in the world for almost four thousand years. And it's still standing! It was built for a pharaoh named Khufu forty-six hundred years ago. It stood more than 480 feet (146 m) high when it was built. More than two million huge limestone blocks were used to build it. Workers had to cut, move, and place every single one!

Ancient Egypt Facts

- Egypt has few trees, so people made buildings from mud bricks hardened by the sun.
- Senet game boards have been found in many ancient Egyptian tombs.
- Scientists who study ancient Egypt are called Egyptologists.
- The language spoken by ancient Egyptians no longer exists.

Glossary

class: someone's rank in society

drought: a long period of time without rain

enslaved: forced to do work for another person without being paid

famine: when a large number of people don't have enough food

monument: a statue or other structure built to honor a person or event

preserve: keep from spoiling

scribe: an ancient Egyptian who was trained to read and write hieroglyphics

society: a large group of people who live and work together

tomb: a burial place for the dead

Learn More

BBC: Who Were the Ancient Egyptians?
https://www.bbc.co.uk/bitesize/articles/zsdpp4j

Britannica Kids: Ancient Egypt
https://kids.britannica.com/students/article/ancient-Egypt/274132

Havemeyer. Janie. *A Day in Ancient Egypt*. Jump!, 2025.

National Geographic Kids: Ancient Egypt
https://kids.nationalgeographic.com/history/article/ancient-egypt

Newbauer, Heidi. *Egyptian Pyramids*. Creative Education, 2025.

Ransom, Candice. *Explore the Aztec Empire*. Lerner Publications, 2026.

Index

Alexander the Great, 19
Anubis, 14

cat, 17

hieroglyphics, 10

Nile River, 4, 7

pharaoh, 13, 20
pyramid, 5, 20

Roman Empire, 19

Photo Acknowledgments

Image credits: Oleh Slobodeniuk/Getty Images, p. 4; duncan1890/Getty Images, pp. 5, 11; Travelpix Ltd/Getty Images, p. 6; Frans Lemmens/Getty Images, p. 7; Leemage/Corbis via Getty Images, p. 8; Laura Westlund/Independent Picture Service, p. 9; Bojan Brecelj/Corbis via Getty Images, p. 10; robyvannucci/Getty Images, p. 12; G. DAGLI ORTI/De Agostini via Getty Images, p. 13; Gunter Reitz/Pix/Michael Ochs Archives/Getty Images, p. 14; Art Images via Getty Images, p. 15; Art Media/Print Collector/Getty Images, p. 16; Heritage Art/Heritage Images via Getty Images, pp. 17, 19; Glowimages/Getty Images, p. 18; sculpies/Getty Images, p. 20.

Cover: Heritage Art/Heritage Images via Getty Images.